WHAT

JOHN COOPER CLARKE shot to prominence in the 1970s as the original 'people's poet'. Rooted in the punk rock ethos, Clarke's poetry intertwines humour, nutty rhymes, obsolete slang and razor-sharp bad language to maximum effect. His unrivalled stage presence and rapid-fire delivery have made his performances legendary in the landscape of modern poetry, while his trademark 'look' continues to resonate with fashionistas young and old. His 2018 collection *The Luckiest Guy Alive*, together with the autobiography *I Wanna Be Yours* (named after his most famous poem), has brought Clarke to a new generation of fans and cemented his position as one of the UK's most influential artists.

ALSO BY JOHN COOPER CLARKE

Ten Years in an Open Necked Shirt

The Luckiest Guy Alive

I Wanna Be Yours

John Cooper Clarke

WHAT

PICADOR

First published 2024 by Picador

This edition first published 2025 by Picador
an imprint of Pan Macmillan
The Smithson, 6 Briset Street, London EC1M 5NR
EU representative: Macmillan Publishers Ireland Ltd, 1st Floor,
The Liffey Trust Centre, 117–126 Sheriff Street Upper,
Dublin 1, D01 YC43
Associated companies throughout the world
www.panmacmillan.com

ISBN 978-1-0350-3319-5

9 8 7 6 5 4 3 2 1

A CIP catalogue record for this book is available from the British Library.

Printed and bound by CPI Group (UK) Ltd, Croydon, CR0 4YY

Quid – me anxius sum?

Contents

WHAT

The Official Guest List

Here's the who's that – are you in it?
Duke McGuinness and his photo finishers
Chandler Burr with a bucket of myrrh
A murderer in human fur
A one man racial slur
Ner ner na ner ner na ner ner
Better not forget her
Charley Davidson and his (yes) Harley Davidson
JR Justice and the VIPs
Anybody who speaks Maltese
Jerry Hall she's very tall
From the Albert Hall at all at all
Rob Lowe – Dr No
Shemp Larry and Moe
Wayne Newton, his sister Fig
Roger Scruton and Mr Big
Kenneth Anger, his sister Coat
Dripping pearls – draped in stoat
The girl with a padlock up the throat
Get Carter, Sam Giancana
Jeffrey Archer and his sudden departure
Clarice Hilton, Little Milton
From East of Sweden, Peter Stilton
Jack Shit and the Zeroes
Borderline unpleasant heroes
Jimmy Zilch and the Scandaleros
Billy Dos Sombreros

Zorba and his Hellenic Shapiros
Sad clown and his tragic pierrots
Prince Baron, the Emperor Ming
Big Ted the Kidney King
El Vengador y los Vengadores
Little Ronaldo, his sister Dolores
Her cakes are very moreish
Admit anybody who knows my brother
But anybody who says she's the mother
Of any child I might have sired
Who ain't my wife and yet she's wired
If you let her in I'm afraid you're fired
I'm mugging you off as I make this mark
Authenticated by Dr John Cooper Clarke

Smooth Operetta

Hopsack with a permacrease
Authorised by the style police
Frogmouth pockets on a flat front
For work or leisure or coming the cunt
When it comes to the classic callards mate
Farahs – since '78

I got a pair in Air Force blue
They look OK with a slip-on shoe
A nice Oxford in a muted plaid
Or a Pringle wouldn't look too bad
You can't pull off a pair of pegs
Farahs – they cover your legs

A carpet knife with double blades
A gamp for when it's damp
Some shades for when the twilight fades
Smooth operetta weekend in Lanzaretta

Neat neat neat neat neat
Please do not make me repeat
The dress code is hard and brief
Look out for the *F* motif
Spick and Spanish borderline sportif
Spotless – alive she cried
Farahs – the parallel stride

Burnley

I'll tell you now and I'll tell you firmly
I don't ever want to go to Burnley
What they do there don't concern me
Why would anybody make the journey

I'll tell you now and I'll tell you flatly
I don't ever want to go to Gatley
I don't even want to go to Batley
Where is that place exactly

Do I want to go to Reddish
I wouldn't visit in a souped-up sheddish
What am I some kind of nebbish
No – I don't want to go to Reddish

I'll tell you now and I'll tell you briefly
I don't ever want to go to Keighley
I'll tell you now just like I told Elsa Lanchester
I don't ever want to go to . . . Newport

Blue Collar Wallah

There's a heteronormative handyman
West of the Fairtrade aisle
He's wearing full-length trousers
And a patriarchal smile
He's shod in manly footwear
His house phone has a dial
He doesn't deal with crank calls
His attitude is on file
He's an old school delinquent
Eating chips and drinking ale
While listening to The Beatles
He oughta be in jail

His obstinate resistance
To every social fad
Keeps him at a distance
But his influence is bad
He could be the plumber
The mechanic or your dad
Smoking his way to an early grave
When he gets there we'll be sad
He's an old school delinquent
With a Cosworth Whale-Tail
He built the world we live in
He oughta be in jail

His emotional illiteracy
Keeps him on the ball
Women crawl all over him
Begging him to call
Round with his pheromonal armpits
And his usefulness and all
They got conscientious heat pumps that
They'd like him to install
All attempts to improve him
Were somehow doomed to fail
Still we can't remove him
He oughta be in jail

Dependable commendable
He's hardly ever broke
Underneath his Harrington
There beats a heart of oak
Give him a messy job
He'll answer okey-doke
He's a Jason Statham lookalike
Let's face it he's a bloke
A bloke who could drink Canada dry
And I don't mean ginger ale
Old school delinquent
He oughta be in jail

His sick sense of humour helps
Where misery is rife
Not for him the Brothers Grim
Or the two-way sporting life

Put your dreams away Jim
He's faithful to his wife
He could take on the world and win
With a clawback hammer and a ratchet knife

With the gift of immortality
He reckons you would find
Life is life whatever
Neither fair nor is it kind
Every previous occupant
Left a mess behind
Plus bad advice is priceless
To a complicated mind
He lives beyond this instant
He's on the treasure trail
Old school delinquent
He oughta be in jail

He's always up for a nice cuppa tea
But he'd rather have a beer
He tried that marijuana once
But it just made everything weird
His bulldog died that's when he cried
A big fat fucking tear
We'll die if we have to DIY
And he could be dead next year
He's a two meat and one veg guy
Potatoes never kale
We can't afford to let him die
He oughta be in jail

Elvis No. 45

Real gone forever he will never grow old
His was a treasure you can measure in gold
Even now he is an image to be sold
But Elvis has left the building

His manly grace his beautiful face
Who could possibly take his place
Look upon that empty space
Elvis has left the building

Time Gentlemen Time

Nature ain't your friend
It's round the fucking bend
It tries to show you constantly
Still you don't comprehend

Time gentlemen time
Will wreck your neck and rip your hip
Break your face and split your lip
Give your spinal column gyp
Help you lose your tenuous grip
On time gentlemen time

Time gentlemen time
Will turn your claret into alligator wine
Put the state of your health on a deadline
Make the seat of your trousers shine
Time gentlemen time

Time gentlemen time
Will fade your gaze when you go online
Will fade you out on the public dime
When it's time gentlemen time

Time gentlemen time will tell you
Nature ain't your friend
Nature made a mess
Nature tries to kill you from day one
With increasing degrees of success

Lydia, Girl with an Itch

Lydia Lydia get rid o' yer chlamydia
Only an idiot would ever consider ya

When dealing with sexual delinquency you have to be inclusive so here's another one on that theme . . .

Necrophilia

Fed up with foreplay and all that palaver
Have a cadaver

R U the Business

Does Superman wear blue tights
And keep away from kryptonite
Do old ladies get mugged at night
R U the business

Do workers want a living wage
Would a tiger run from an open cage
Is turquoise known as Indian beige
R U the business

R U the fuck off business
Is my first name John
Is Strangeways full of prisoners
Am I over twenty-one

Are the royal family rich
Is Scooby Doo one son-of-a-bitch
Is Wembley Stadium a football pitch
R U the business

Did Pablo Escobar knock out coke
Does Batman wear the jagged cloak
Was Jesus Christ a decent bloke
R U the business

Did Oliver Reed ever get pissed
Can Chubby Checker do the twist
Was Karl Marx a communist
R U the business

Was James Dean a cool cat
Was Kennedy a democrat
Do Hasidic men wear hats
R U the business

Will narcotics get you on the hook
Did Dostoyevsky write the odd book
Was Al Capone a bit of a crook
R U the business

Did Buddy Holly wear horn-rimmed specs
Is the Czech Republic full of Czechs
Did Sigmund Freud consider sex
R U the business

Did Adolf Hitler dislike Jews
Jesus gypsies fags and booze
And were his catamites born to lose
R U the business

Did Elvis ever rock 'n' roll
Did James Brown have any soul
Would I touch you with a ten-foot barge pole
R U the business

Tribute to the Late Sir Peter O'Sullevan

We're seven eighths of the way through a seven horse
race and it's Shoofly Medicine Box and Crockery Barn from
Drumlargan Junior and Grandmaster Slash with Dobbin
and Clippity Clop as the twin back markers

we're coming up to the seventh furlong from home marker
now and it's still Shoofly in front with Medicine Box testing
positive in hot pursuit as Drumlargan Junior relegates
Crockery Barn to fourth place then in the sheepskin noseband
it's Dobbin giving trouble for Grandmaster Slash as Clippity
Clop shows a late burst of stamina on the stand side

now as we approach the finish it's Clippity Clop several
lengths in front of Shoofly with Dobbin in third place and
Drumlargan Junior and Grandmaster Slash and Crockery Barn
and finally Medicine Box and there'll be some suicidal turf
accountants up and down the high streets of the British Isles
tonight over to Peter Bromley in the winner's enclosure

also in honour of Simon Bazalgette, Fred Done, Sir Henry Cecil, Jock Scott and Barry Dennis aka The Romford Foghorn, without whom . . .

Clown Town

A place to develop a nervous stutter
Or an indiscriminate pain
Walking in the gutter
But gazing at the drains
Under heavy manners encased in dread
Feet don't leave the ground
There's a gangland scrap yard dead ahead
Clown Town

Uptown Mr Noun town
Downtown Doctor Brown town
Upside-down frown town
Dancing with the sound down
You look like you've been around
Clown Town

I know this place like the back of my neck
Each unsuspected street
Where a deal gets the seal of a gentleman's cheque
And words like 'safe' and 'sweet'
Saying it is don't make it the case
And wishing it was don't count
Strapped up? Stuck for space?
Clown Town

On the wide side of the big divide
It's narrow looks and snide asides
The nightlife ain't so dandified
Damned if I know where you're gonna hide
When liquefied inside

'Any old iron' a rent man croons
In a faintly desperate tone
Downhill from the 70s boom
It's the soft shoe shuffle home
The fat lady lost her voice
The show boat runs aground
Who would be here out of choice
Clown Town

I couldn't see why just by being there
I could be looking like a sap
All I could see was a middle-European
With a puzzled expression and a map
No comfort in the knowledge
The knowledge ain't that sound
A fake diploma from a tinpot college
Clown Town

Uptown Mr Noun town
Downtown Dr Brown town
Upside-down frown town
Dancing with the sound down
You look like you've been around
Clown Town

Lines Upon the Death of Mr Bruce Reynolds

28.02.2013

The dread hand of Mr Grief
Can fall upon the shoulder like an autumn leaf
But then the light touch was his leitmotif
Here's a rhyme in the office of a wreath

81 years and all too brief
81 tears of sweet relief
81 beers and here's to the chief
RIP the gentleman thief

Acknowledgement: Nick Reynolds

Losers

Twenty-one people smoking in the rain
Outside an empty boozer
From here and there and back they came
Like some kinda losers

Across the road a parade of shops
A barbers a bookies and a Burger King
Where I knew this spiv whose tips were tops
But now he's never heard a thing
You can't go back to from where you came
Is my advice to you sir
Chain chain chain smoking in the rain
Like some kinda loser

There is a void in the exile heart
And nature hates a hoover
If you don't smoke yet don't start
Outside that empty boozer
Like some kinda loser

The drink trade's useful idiots beam
Like fellow travellers and cruisers
At the dwindling band of cigarette fiends
Outside some empty boozer
Back-a-yard where the ambulance screams
Like some kinda loser

Across the road that parade of shops
With a nail bar and a small claims brief
A sideline in discount chops
With serving suggestions overleaf
Soaking wet these pictures of regret
Regard their shrunken future
Hacking into a towelette
Outside some empty boozer
Freezing cold in an all over sweat
Like some kinda loser

Dream Home Ghetto

Room number blue – apartment A
The whole town's on holiday
I'm going no place
I'm living in a show place
A dream home ghetto

Hands off the threads creep
This level of luxury don't come cheap
When do we sleep
I get my bread from a cake boutique
No pressure on the street

The gates give out on a rancorous air
Despair and disrepair
There's a sky lounge I'll take you there
Somewhere – in the dream home ghetto

People try to sell you stuff
You only think you wanna buy
You reach out to the outside world
Each time you wanna cry

Toodle pip – I'll help you pack
I'll be right here when you get back
Here where things are kinda slack
In fact a dream home ghetto

There is a social roadblock
Where the brakes are set to screech
You can keep Utopia Parkway
And stick your Cameo Beach

Here is an avenue of visible worth
It's quite the nicest place on earth
Go ride the wild surf
And I'll take this dream home ghetto

There's a balconette for a Juliet
And a place to hang your fishing net
How continental can you get
You bet – it's a dream home ghetto

The nearest neighbour is a guy with a gut
A muumuu and a German attack mutt
But we got gates that stay real shut
A dream home ghetto

So room number blue – apartment A
The whole town's on holiday
I'm going no place
I'm living in a show place
A dream home ghetto
One more time this time with echo
A dream home ghetto

Thug

You see him through that lavender mist
Freaked out in the fug
In his eyes you are trouble as he
Gives your braids a vicious little tug
He greets every tragedy with a non-committal shrug
He's citizen X he ain't complex
He's a thug

You think he's just a big lug
A naughty boy in need of a hug
And life could be sweet and safe and snug
If only he'd stop keep pulling out the rug
He's got the bad bad bad bad bad bad bad bad bug
He's a thug

If his best friend is a forty-four slug
If he drinks raw gravy right out of the jug
If the family motto is glug glug glug
He's a thug

If to him every man with a smile on his face is smug
If he tells you his name is Pancho when really his name is Doug
If everybody but him is a useful mug
If he blocks up your airways with a second-hand butt plug
He's wrong and strange he'll never change
He's a thug

Stay Outta Jail Gaz

Hang your hoodie on a handy hook
Help yourself to a self-help book
Teach yourself to cook
I know your sisters and they ain't crooks

Stay outta jail Gaz
Stay outta jail
Because losers lose and failures fail
Stay outta jail

Ease up on the drugs and booze
Lazer off those bad tattoos
Keep your mug shot off the news
Walk in someone else's shoes

Why trudge that troublesome trail
Stay outta jail Gaz
Stay outta jail

Wear your cap the right way round
Tuck your shirt in go to town
Get a job and hold it down
Put your life on the rebound

For a happy end to a cautionary tale
Stay outta jail you cunt
Stay outta jail

Anger Manager Anger Manager

Woke up in town by a sudden pang
I heard casual oaths in military slang
Any conversation would have to hang
Bang bang bang bang bang
Anger manager anger manager

I woke up in town but I can't expand
On the broken bottle in either hand
I got reasons but they're never gonna stand
Anger manager anger manager

I woke up in town there was a car crash
Shards of glass and all that trash
Call that driving I could give it a bash
But I'd only get rahassed
Too bad it coulda been a blast
Anger manager anger manager

Bang bang what's that sound
I woke up in town with a crowd around
A gin hound found in an ugly mound
You put me straight you gave me the lowdown

With the self-restraint of a rank amateur
I lost my rag and I really hammered ya
Word is I nearly spannered ya
Anger manager anger manager

I lived in a crowd I could never be buried alone
Anger manager anger manager please let me take you home

Ode to the Coast

A big fat sky and a thousand shrieks
The tide arrives and the timber creaks
A world away from the working week
Oú est la vie nautique?
That's where the sea comes in

Dishevelled shells and shovelled sands
Architecture all unplanned
A spade 'n' bucket Disneyland
A golden space a Frisbee and
The kids and dogs can run and run
And not run into anyone
Way out! Real gone!
That's where the sea comes in

The sea has never been friend to man
Joseph Conrad said it
The accomplice to human restlessness
It'll kill you when it's ready

Impervious to human speech
Idle time and tidal reach
Some memories you can't impeach
A nice cuppa splosh and a round of toast
A cursory glance at the morning post
A pointless walk along the coast
That's what floats my boat the most
That's where the sea comes in

Now voyager – once resigned
Go forth to seek and find
The hazy days you left behind
Right there in the back of your mind
Where lucid dreams begin
With rolling dunes and rattling shale
The shoreline then a swollen sail
Picked out by a shimmering halo
That's where the sea comes in
Could this be luck by chance
Eternity in a second glance
A universe beyond romance
That's where the sea comes in
Yes – that's where the sea comes in

Thank you Yankee Bill

Elvis No. 46

The King is 46 years dead
And yet he will survive
In my heart if not my head
He will remain alive
Opinions are optional
I've heard a few
But if you don't love Elvis Presley
There's something wrong with you

Dekko Beach

There's a lilac bus that leaves at dusk
In a cloud of dusty pink
It leaves behind the scent of musk
Exactly as you'd think

So wipe the germ-free surfaces
With another coat of bleach
Here is where the surface is
Dekko Beach

The sherbet shade of the esplanade
Its creamy coloured curves
And its linear fenestration
Are a tonic for that twisted nerve

It's a plutocrat's palazzo
Painted pastel peach
But what's it to ya Fatso
This is Dekko Beach

Turn up the Streisand
And pepper up your speech
It's like some decadent dessert island
Dekko Beach

Beware of Legionnaires' disease
The place is just too clean
If the ten commandments bring you peace
It's not gonna be your scene
There has to be a line in the sand
But it's way out of reach
Where your wildest dreams get out of hand
Dekko Beach

I told yer I told yer when I seen that effeminate soldier
Noel Coward, Cole Porter
And the thoughts of Chairman Nietzsche
Couldn't pour any cold water on
Dekko Beach

Just a bong to highlight
That time to cut some slack
Just a thong at twilight a twanging from its crack
It's Adam and Steve and Madame and Eve
Once more into the breach
You better make your excuses and leave
Dekko Beach

Incremental shades of dark
A high vanilla moon
Sunset over flamingo park
And the nightingales begin to croon

Whatever it's a question of
You answer with a screech
As you head in the vague direction of
Dekko Beach

With visions of adultery
Clogging up their mind
Where drinking is compulsory
Everybody gets blind
With the seven deadly sins on sale
For a couple of shekels each
How can it possibly fail
Dekko Beach

For George, Son of the Mailman

One day a fellow named George
Found a suit of clothes in a gorge (what's the chances)
Inside the coat
Was a farewell note
With a signature no one could forge

That's all there is that rhymes with George – take it from a professional, I've got a rhyming dictionary. Why didn't he call him Jack? I could have done an 8 pager (and this is also why I've never written a poem to my late father)

Doomed

In long pants I feel over-styled
I look at a dog I see a blind child
I look at a car I see a planet defiled
Where the summer time is a burning hell
In the wound up webbed up whereabouts where the worried
well dwell

Do tell
We dwell on whether stress could lead to suicidal thoughts
We dwell on the blatant judgementalism that still persists in
the courts
Everybody I know agrees with me
The worried well are worried well we would be wouldn't we

Sugarfree sugar that's up my street
The real stuff is just too sweet
And do we really need to eat
The poisons that they sell
From this tainted and ungrateful soil
Where the worried well dwell

We dwell on that long litigious procession
About to bill us all
We dwell on the so-called medical profession
Who are trying to kill us all
Everybody I know agrees with me
The worried well are worried well we would be wouldn't we

I'll show you skid row in a can of beer
And a future that holds only doubt and fear
With any luck we'll be dead next year
Before the boiling oceans swell
This is the grim consensus where the worried well dwell

We dwell upon the problems caused by living for so long
We like to put things right before they're wrong
Everybody I know agrees with me
The worried well are worried well we would be wouldn't we

Storms of protest floods of tears
A tidal wave of social engineers
For years and years and years and years
Ye gods and bloody hell
Poetry falls on deafened ears
Where the worried well dwell

Diez Macarenas

It ain't what you do it's the way that you do it
It ain't what you do it's the way that you do it
It ain't what you do it's the way that you do it
Hey
Macarena

I heard the word again today
And I wondered why it ever went away
I thought it was here to stay
Like Ricky Martin or Fernando Rey
Like yay yay and gabba gabba hey
Hey
Macarena

One maca two maca three Macarena
Four maca five maca six Macarena
Seven maca eight maca nine Macarena
DIEZ
Macarenas

From the Marginal Pre-dawn Schedules

I wrote this when a Granada Television programme called Taxi Nights *(available on pre-dawn schedules) was enjoying a re-run. It's a kinda 'fly in the cab' dashcam documentary about the Curry Mile, which is like an Asian-style Vegas.*

Drunk chicks blow chunks out the back of a stretch
Staccato heels a-clatter
Rogue male post-Ramadan revellers on a rapture
On this aromatic mile the moral high ground gets overcrowded
 some times

Gold frankincense and murder
Social worker in a burqa
What a party this nearly is
Nine kinds of in-store fizz
Not one a colour that is
Rainbow syrup in nylon frizz

Gold frankincense and murder
Social worker in a burqa
Three blind drunks in a tête-à-tête-à-tête
Details draped in mild regret
Scrawled on the back of a serviette

Gymnasium clothes that wouldn't look out of place in a
gymnasium
Ratner chains and a partially gelatinated spike job
Clamp-handed Morlocks of the planet Zonk
Zombie goons from nowhere
Honk if you heart jeepsters
Skinhead queen with a 'fuck shit up' neck violation
Earshot of the Bangalanga Station

Gold frankincense and murder
Social worker in a burqa
What a party this nearly is
First there is a taxi then there is no taxi then there is . . . no taxi

A glittering film of crystal sweat
Patinates those features yet
A fallen shadow a neon minaret
Call the cops they ain't here yet
You're only as good as your last cigarette
I would remember the street would forget

You Don’t Get It Every Week

You don’t get it every week
It’s utterly unique
What is this dish of which I speak
Boxing Day Bubble and Squeak

Home Honey I'm High

Frontal lobes just get a trim
Or did you meet the Moonies

Wrong on both counts Jim
Tee many martoonies

Too Hot 4 Hoxton Too Kool 4 Skool

If ever he was dressed in vogue
It's because some wide boy tricked him
Suddenly it's Alf Mullins
Hipster fashion victim

Sir Tom Jones

Back in town in the black Rolls Royce
The funky hunky housewives' choice
In one fact he can rejoice
His trousers don't affect his voice

Rolling News Blues

BBC – the daily *Guardian* – you choose
This misery soup is on a loop
Rolling news blues

There's nice people doing nice things
Most of the time
I can't prove it but you gotta believe me
You wouldn't hear it on the public dime

BBC – the daily *Guardian* – you choose
Deep concern could only earn you the
Rolling news blues

There's never been a better time to be alive
Gratitude is de rigueur
You used to be finished at sixty-five
Now it's triple figures

There's one thing fucks it up
Like gravel in your shoes
The horror the horror that makes the cut
On the rolling news blues

Hawkeye Magoo

Dial 9 for an outside line
That's the rule that suits me fine
I should have seen the signs
Hawkeye Magoo
I only ever saw what I wanted to

Hawkeye Magoo—my manners are refined
I lost my specs I couldn't go anywhere
I was practically blind
And, believe me, I've been stuck in there
And I haven't got a beautiful mind

My first wife cheated on me once
My first response was nonchalance
I came off looking like a bit of a ponce
Hawkeye Magoo
I only ever saw what I wanted to

I had a dope habit I was happy as a clown
I was a monochrome guy in a technicolor town
Or the other way round
Whatever

My TV is a house of Hollywood smiles
Kojak, The Simpsons and *The Rockford Files*
Leave it – don't touch those dials
Hawkeye Magoo
I only ever saw what I wanted to

I'll clock the cut of a criminal's coat
Or a dotted line across the throat
But I didn't anticipate Raoul Moat
Hawkeye Magoo
I only ever saw what I wanted to

Lights Kamera Achtung

From the orange groves of Spitalfields to the vineyards of
St Pauls
Horror Clown by Megahertz is bouncing off the walls
Kraut metal is the sound track that gets you on the total wire
Echoes echo echoes and there's an amplifier fire
The heat the heat the blasted heat o qué ca-fucking-lor
Bring on the inferno! More I tell you more
Like a Ray Lowry nightmare the dress code's black on black
We stole our children's future we're never gonna give it back
Never never never never never, Jack, not this side of a
Marshall Stack
This ain't my kinda music but I like it anyway
We're the de-generation we got something to say
At the annual Krautrock special
Shitloads of death metal

Beatnik Empire

Beatnik Empire
Emperor bigshot
You had to be there
Mellow but shit hot
Beatnik Empire
Death to the robots
Blue jeans a peacoat
And a Brooks Brothers shirt on
It cost me a C-note
That put the hurt on
But when do we live
Pray tell me I know not
Beatnik Empire
Death to the robot

Beatnik Empire
Get out and stay out
Get with it Clyde
And I mean like way out
A cranked up car chase
That ends in a road block
Beatnik Empire
Death to the robot

Beatnik empire
Betrayed by the bongos
Preston Epps
And the Royal King Combo
Chin strap face fuzz
Sloppy but so what
Beatnik Empire
Death to the robot

A bottle of schoolboy
Under the soapbox
Beatnik Empire
Death to the robot

The Slums of Belgravia

Part One

Trouble in Paradise? You bet
Why not suffer in luxury as marriages made in the morbid bowels of purgatory sink into the self-harming moral swamp of the lumpen bourgeoisie
With hilarious results

Part Two: In Praise of Shame

Your PR guy can't help you now with any amount of spin
The soul is not a butterfly to be inspected on a pin
Show me one immortal soul that isn't smeared with sin
That won't be washed away by a thunderstorm of gin
If your heart was your home you wouldn't let your sister in
We make the laws and the get-out clauses don't you worry Jim
Make a firm purpose of amendment – look within

The Marital Miseries of the Modern Misogynist Male *or* The Rime of the Ancient Marrier

From the doghouse to the cat flap
And back again without a map
He could be heading for a slap
His fractured fairytale gone zap
Just like I said was gonna happen
She hoovers when he tries to take a nap
In the manner of Andy Capp
She sold his Frogeye Sprite for scrap
Step lively mind the gap
Some day he's gonna snap
Who would be a chap
She fucks up he takes the rap
Like any penis-owning sap
He fell into her sugary trap
Now he's taking all that crap
That drops in daily right on tap
He's got a lockdown dog going yap yap yap
You don't believe me consult the app
Who would be who would be
I ask you two times make that three
Some day he's gonna snap
Who would be a chap

Mr Hyde and Mr Hyde

Each dawn at the death of the moon
Just me and my mad shadow in a room
No sunshine any time soon
Since Dr Jekyll died
It's Mr Hyde and Mr Hyde

From the back of an unremarkable car
Hanging out with my eyelids ajar
Hey kid – wanna go to Mars
With a mad scientist on the slide
Mr Hyde and Mr Hyde

Affection gave you a limited scope
It allowed your heart to harbour hope
You gotta be on some kind of dope
I mean what a fucking rotter
I don't have a good side
Mr Hyde and Mr Hyde

Sheffield

Written for Arctic Monkeys to the tune of 'Stockport' by Frankie Vaughan

I've travelled up and down this country
From St Helens down to St Ives
I've dined in the finest of places
And there's one word I read on the knives
Displayed on any blade of quality
Sheffield Sheffield Sheffield
It calls to me

I'm going to Sheffield
I really rate it
I mean Sheffield
I'm gonna reiterate it
S-H-E-F-F-I-E-L-D
Sheffield Sheffield Sheffield
It's got to be

There's Richard Hawley on the corner
The Cockers both Jarvis and Joe
Henderson's relish to order
And a steak and kidney to go
Park Hill's airborne avenues above
Sheffield – that's the place I love

I'm going to Sheffield
The reputation is stainless
Oh yeah Sheffield
Internationally famous
Where hobnail boots are shabby chic
And Wednesday ain't just some lousy day of the week
S-H-E-F-F-I-E-L-D
Sheffield Sheffield Sheffield
Shoo be doo bee do-eee

Maybe it ain't that pretty
But it kinda gets under your skin
This heavy industrial city
Of railroads and razors and pins
A heart of solid steel pulsates within
Sheffield Sheffield Sheffield
Gets some in

I'm going to Sheffield
My destiny walks here
You heard me right Sheffield
Republic of South Yorkshire
It's a town that's out on its own
I'm gonna scream it down this microphone
SHEFFIELD MY SECOND HOME
SWEET SWINGIN' HOME